This journal belongs to

_____

*Living Expressions* invites you to explore God's Word and express your creativity in ways that are refreshing to the spirit and restorative to the soul.

**LIVING
EXPRESSIONS**
COLLECTION

Visit Tyndale at www.tyndale.com.

*Tyndale Momentum* and the Tyndale Momentum logo are registered trademarks of Tyndale House Publishers, Inc. *Living Expressions* is a trademark of Tyndale House Publishers, Inc. Tyndale Momentum is an imprint of Tyndale House Publishers, Inc., Carol Stream, Illinois.

*Gratitude: A Prayer and Praise Coloring Journal*

Prayers adapted by Amie Carlson from *365 Pocket Prayers for Mothers*, copyright © 2014 by Barton-Veerman Company, Amie Carlson, and Erin Keeley Marshall. All rights reserved. Additional text copyright © 2016 by Amie Carlson.

Cover illustrations are the properties of their respective copyright holders, and all rights are reserved: flowers © Mia Charro/Creative Market; pineapple © Felicity French; graphic frame © marushabelle/Creative Market. Interior illustrations are the properties of their respective copyright holders, and all rights are reserved: p 6–7 floral pattern © Maria Galybina/Creative Market; p 14–15, 58–59 mandala © Artem Demidenko/Ckybe's Corner/Creative Market; p 18–19 plants © Julia Vyazovskaya/Creative Market; p 21 rays © Ardian Radityo/TSV Creative/Creative Market; p 22–23 summer icons © Callie Hegstrom/Make Media Co/Creative Market; p 26–27, 40–41 swirls © Varvara Kurakina/Depiano/Creative Market; p 36–37 magnolia © Ksenia Lokko/Creative Market; p 38 bird © Erin I/Trinket Allsorts/Creative Market; p 52–53 digital paper © Almazia Pratita/Popuri Design/Creative Market and flower © Evgeniya Ivanova/Creative Market; p 84–85 flowers © Alexandra Dzhiganskaya/Creative Market; p 94–95 love dingbats © 3lines/Creative Market; p 98–99 flower pattern © Darya Gribovskaya/Creative Market.

Designed by Jennifer Ghionzoli

Edited by Anisa Baker

Scripture quotations are taken from the *Holy Bible*, New Living Translation, copyright © 1996, 2004, 2015 by Tyndale House Foundation. Used by permission of Tyndale House Publishers, Inc., Carol Stream, Illinois 60188. All rights reserved.

ISBN 978-1-4964-1579-0

Printed in China

22   21   20   19   18   17   16
7    6    5    4    3    2    1

# introduction

**WELCOME!** Are you ready to CONNECT with God in a *fresh*, new way through the written word and prayer? The art of creative expression provides a wonderful outlet for *relaxing* and destressing. In addition to praying and reading the Scriptures, activities like coloring, journaling, and drawing offer effective ways for giving thanks to God and *deepening* your faith. Meditating on Scripture can be taken to an entirely new level when you add color and INNER CREATIVITY to the process.

As you enter into these prayers, take it slow. Spend time thinking about what you are saying to God. You may even want to *personalize* each prayer to reflect the needs and hopes you have for your own life. To make these moments with God more meaningful, write down your own prayers and petitions and *color* the artwork or *create* your own drawing. Let this experience take you to an entirely new level of connection with God. Suggestions are added along the way to further inspire you in this time of *quiet reflection* and prayer. Don't worry about the end result; LET GOD INSPIRE YOU and lead the way as you allow yourself to fully experience *gratitude*.

# friends

## TRAVEL THE ROAD TOGETHER

God,

You created me for community, and I'm so grateful for friends who fill my life with love and laughter. Help me to *be* a good friend. Open my eyes to those around me—perhaps a new coworker or the young woman I just met at the park—who may be lonely and in need of a friend. Help me to show your love to others.

*You didn't choose me. I chose you.*
*I appointed you to go and produce lasting fruit, so that the*
*Father will give you whatever you ask for, using my name.*
*This is my command: Love each other.*

JOHN 15:16-17

# Love each other

# OUR POWERFUL AND CREATIVE GOD

God,

I marvel at your majesty and imagination. You spoke into creation such fine nuances and complex details, from the perfectly shaped fingernails on a tiny baby to the vivid colors of an evening sunset. I am so proud to call you my heavenly Father. Please give me the boldness to tell someone about your matchless power today.

*O Sovereign LORD!*
*You made the heavens and earth by your*
*strong hand and powerful arm.*
*Nothing is too hard for you!*

JEREMIAH 32:17

# NOTHING IS TOO HARD FOR YOU!

# CHERISH
*every moment*

· · · · · · · · · · · · · · · · · · · · · · · · ·

*Lord,*
Please weave into my days moments that cause
me to stand in awe of you. Help me to rejoice in
the wonder of your ways. Increase my enjoyment
of you when my heart has become jaded. Thank
you, God, for surprising me with your glory and
splendor. Thank you for the ability to see how
common people and experiences can actually
prove to be quite glorious.

*Everyone was gripped with great wonder*
*and awe, and they praised God, exclaiming,*
*"We have seen amazing things today!"*

LUKE 5:26

.......................................................................

.......................................................................

.......................................................................

.......................................................................

.......................................................................

AMAZING...
WONDERFUL...
PRAISE
GOD!

# I choose LOVE today

Use this space to draw some of your favorite things—for example, flowers, birds, hearts, or butterflies. You can also write down characteristics you appreciate about God, your family, or your friends.

8

GOD loves YOU & HAS Chosen YOU

1 THESSALONIANS 1:4

# the Ultimate Promise Keeper!

*Heavenly Father,*

When I long to feel protected in the midst of change and unknowns, I dwell on your commitment to me. You keep your promises to watch over me and my family because we are yours. As I focus on your unchanging guard, I am changed. My faith is boosted and my fears are soothed. Thank you for staying true to all the pledges you have made.

*He will cover you with his feathers.*
*He will shelter you with his wings.*
*His faithful promises are your armor and protection.*

PSALM 91:4

# He will shelter you

_____

_____

_____

_____

_____

_____

_____

_____

_____

_____

_____

_____

_____

_____

_____

_____

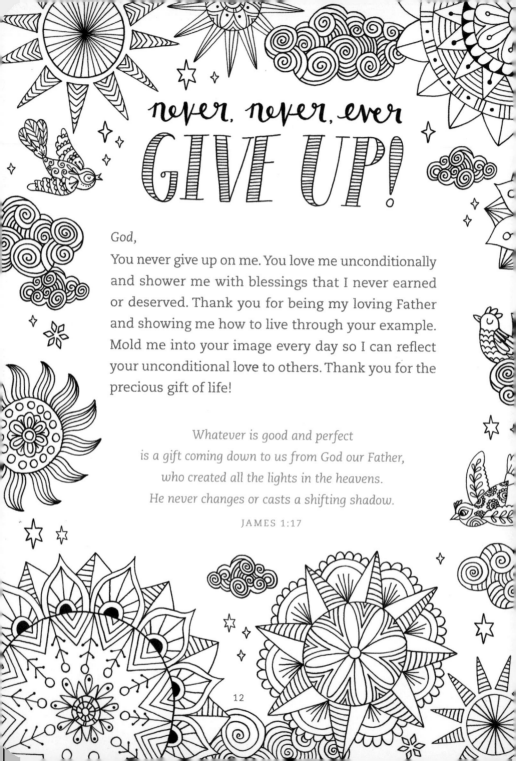

# never, never, ever GIVE UP!

God,

You never give up on me. You love me unconditionally and shower me with blessings that I never earned or deserved. Thank you for being my loving Father and showing me how to live through your example. Mold me into your image every day so I can reflect your unconditional love to others. Thank you for the precious gift of life!

*Whatever is good and perfect*
*is a gift coming down to us from God our Father,*
*who created all the lights in the heavens.*
*He never changes or casts a shifting shadow.*

JAMES 1:17

# he NEVER changes

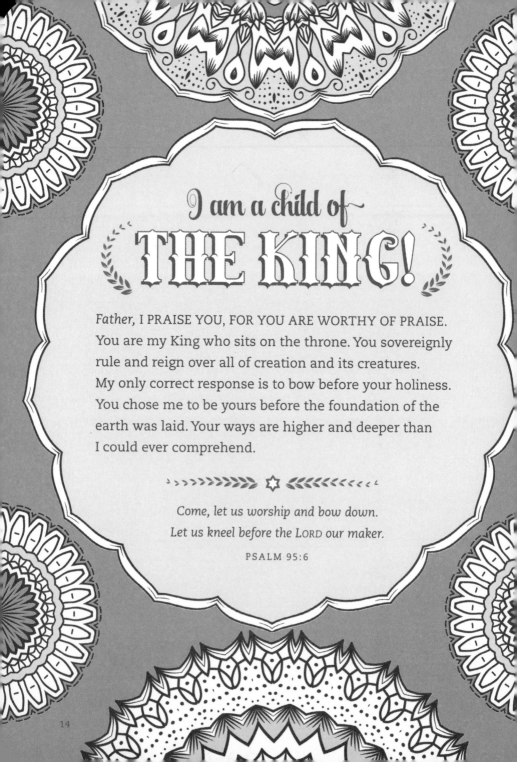

# I am a child of
# THE KING!

Father, I PRAISE YOU, FOR YOU ARE WORTHY OF PRAISE.
You are my King who sits on the throne. You sovereignly
rule and reign over all of creation and its creatures.
My only correct response is to bow before your holiness.
You chose me to be yours before the foundation of the
earth was laid. Your ways are higher and deeper than
I could ever comprehend.

*Come, let us worship and bow down.*
*Let us kneel before the LORD our maker.*

PSALM 95:6

Come, let us
# WORSHIP

I am grateful

Draw or sketch some of the people and things you are grateful for.

# *The first duty of love is to* LISTEN

Lord,

Thank you for the image in your Word of you bending down to listen to me. I'm drawn to love you more. Thank you for listening to me, for drawing near when I call to you. Knowing you want to help me makes such a difference in my hope. Please grow my heart to offer that kind of acceptance and comfort to others when they hurt.

*Because he bends down to listen,*
*I will pray as long as I have breath!*

PSALM 116:2

I will pray!

GIVING IT MY BEST

Father,

You have a plan for my life and for using the talents and skills you have given me. Help me remember that you want me to give my best to every task and trust that you will reward me someday for my efforts to live for you. Please grant me a spirit of gratefulness and remind me that I am a living demonstration of your love.

*Be strong and immovable.*
*Always work enthusiastically for the Lord,*
*for you know that nothing*
*you do for the Lord is ever useless.*

1 CORINTHIANS 15:58

Be Strong

LOVE

# ✳ FRIENDS ARE THE

## *Family*

## I HAVE CHOSEN

*God,*

I am so thankful for my faithful and devoted friends. Their generous acts of love and service overwhelm my heart. Because they have been sensitive to your promptings, you have used them to meet some of my greatest needs. Dear Lord, please give them an extra measure of your blessing for the many ways they have blessed me.

*There is no greater love
than to lay down one's life for one's friends.*

JOHN 15:13

NO GREATER **Love**

_____

_____

_____

_____

_____

_____

_____

_____

_____

I give you thanks, O Lord

PSALM 138:1

Engage in gratefulness by meditating on Psalm 138:1
while writing it repeatedly in the space below.

LEARN FROM *Yesterday,*

LIVE FOR *today,*

HOPE FOR *tomorrow*

Lord,

If I put my trust in you, you promise to be my rock and my refuge. This is the source of my hope and the origin of true joy. Remind me again today to be grateful for this promise and thankful for the blessings you have given me. Help me to rejoice in your overflowing goodness to me.

*I pray that God, the source of hope,*
*will fill you completely with joy and peace because*
*you trust in him. Then you will overflow with confident hope*
*through the power of the Holy Spirit.*

ROMANS 15:13

# God, THE SOURCE OF hope

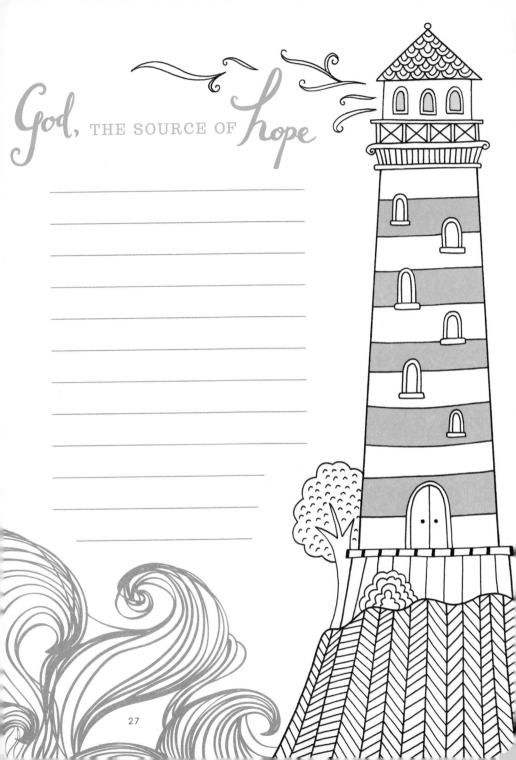

# Set your life on FIRE

Lord,

I long to know you and serve you. Give me grace to follow the holy practices you have shown me that are for my growth in grace. Nurture in me the habit of daily time at your feet so that I might become the person you are calling me to be. Thank you for refining me.

*I will bring [them] through the fire and make them pure.*
*I will refine them like silver and purify them like gold.*
*They will call on my name, and I will answer them.*

ZECHARIAH 13:9

# Call on my name

_____

_____

_____

_____

_____

_____

_____

_____

_____

_____

_____

_____

### OUR GOD IS AN
# AWESOME GOD!

*God,*

You are Yahweh, the Great I Am. You created the heavens, the stars, and the earth. You cause mountains to move and kingdoms to rise and tumble. At your command, people's best-laid plans are changed to conform to your will. In your compassion, you forgive repentant sinners, heal the sick, and set the lonely in families. You are Savior, Healer, almighty Warrior, tender Comforter . . . GOD. Thank you for being my everything.

*God is my helper. The Lord keeps me alive!*

PSALM 54:4

# GOD IS MY HELPER

Close your eyes and be still. In the space below, draw any pictures or record any thoughts or reflections that come to mind.

BE STILL AND KNOW THAT I AM GOD!

PSALM 46:10

# Simple pleasures are life's treasures

Heavenly Father,

I woke up this morning with a light heart. You have certainly showered your blessings on me lately. Simple pleasures like baking, singing, and chatting with friends fill me with joy. The memories of these last few weeks are already making me smile. I know life will not always be this smooth, but I am so grateful for the harmony in my life right now.

*I have learned how to be content with whatever I have.*

PHILIPPIANS 4:11

# Be content

# Get your praise on!

*Lord,* Today as I walk through the beauty of your creation, I am overcome by all your goodness to me. You have filled my heart to overflowing with thankfulness for all you have given me—breath, life, and good gifts too many to count. May the first words on my lips be praise to you. Let the praise of your name fill my home.

*I will praise the Lord at all times.*
*I will constantly speak his praises.*

PSALM 34:1

# LOVED, CALLED & CHOSEN BY GOD

*Heavenly Father,*

Today I am celebrating the fact that I am your precious child. You have chosen me as your own. You died for my sins and invited me to experience life with you. Thank you for loving me. Let me live today in the joy that comes from knowing that I am yours forever.

*Work hard to prove that you really are among those God has called and chosen. Do these things, and you will never fall away.*

2 PETER 1:10

# YOU ARE CALLED & CHOSEN

# WORRIES THAT KEEP ME FROM GOD

Make a list of what causes you to worry—or cut out pictures
that represent those things and paste them in a collage.
Give them to God in prayer.

# happiness is a JOURNEY, ~not a destination~

Heavenly Father,

Hearing the giggles of children as they run and play reminds me of what happiness truly is. Thank you for giving me a tangible reminder of your joy in my life. Help me to take the time to play and enjoy life today. May I live each moment with sweet abandon, remembering that my life is in your hands.

*Let the heavens be glad, and the earth rejoice!*
*Tell all the nations, "The LORD reigns!"*
*Let the sea and everything in it shout his praise!*
*Let the fields and their crops burst out with joy!*

1 CHRONICLES 16:31-32

The LORD Reigns!

_____

_____

_____

_____

_____

_____

_____

_____

_____

_____

# GRACE *changes everything*

Lord,

I am grateful for the gift of your grace. You know me inside and out, and you see everything I do. When I miss the mark, you extend forgiveness without heaping shame on my head. Thank you for walking with me as I navigate life's mountains and valleys. Thanks for believing in me and loving me despite my flaws. Help me extend that same grace to others.

*[The Lord] said, "My grace is all you need.*
*My power works best in weakness."*
*So now I am glad to boast about my weaknesses,*
*so that the power of Christ can work through me.*

2 CORINTHIANS 12:9

my GRACE is all you need

# Celebrate
## EVERYDAY MOMENTS

Jesus,

How wonderful it is that those who know you as Savior have a reason to celebrate each day. In fact, you provide countless reasons to live with a joy-filled heart. Please help me model this grateful attitude to the people in my life so they will be reminded to keep an eternal perspective—especially when circumstances are difficult.

*You will show me the way of life, granting me the joy of your presence and the pleasures of living with you forever.*

PSALM 16:11

THE joy of YOUR PRESENCE

# I CONFESS . . .

Using a pencil, make a list of your sins in the space below.
Then erase them—just like God erases your sins when he forgives you.

# EVERY DAY IS A NEW OPPORTUNITY TO BLESS OTHERS

Lord,

Thank you for the reminder that all my interactions with others either offer hope and encouragement or miss the chance to do so. When my mood is low, please fill me with your grace. I don't want to miss the opportunity to act as your merciful, thoughtful child and make a positive difference in someone's life.

*Let's not get tired of doing what is good.*
*At just the right time we will reap a harvest*
*of blessing if we don't give up.*

GALATIANS 6:9

---

---

---

---

---

# *Every day starts with a* CLEAN SLATE

. . . . . . . . . . . . . . . . . . . . . . . . . . . . .

*Lord Jesus,*

You know what I am thankful for today? Despite the hurts and disappointments in this life, I have your promise that one day tears, pain, and suffering will be no more. Even though life seems chaotic and unruly right now, you are still on the throne. You are making all things new. Thank you!

*The one sitting on the throne said,*
*"Look, I am making everything new!"*
*And then he said to me, "Write this down,*
*for what I tell you is trustworthy and true."*

**REVELATION 21:5**

. . . . . . . . . . . . . . . . . . . . . . . . . . . . . . . . . . . . . . . . . . . . . . . . . . .

. . . . . . . . . . . . . . . . . . . . . . . . . . . . . . . . . . . . . . . . . . . . . . . . . . .

. . . . . . . . . . . . . . . . . . . . . . . . . . . . . . . . . . . . . . . . . . . . . . . . . . .

. . . . . . . . . . . . . . . . . . . . . . . . . . . . . . . . . . . . . . . . . . . . . . . . . . .

I am making everything
NEW!

DANCE *like* NO ONE *is* WATCHING

Lord,

There is nothing quite like watching children dance with exuberance. Their innocent pleasure in the smallest of delights touches me and reminds me that I need to experience more joy in my life. Help me take the time to stop and be grateful for blessings you have given me. Help me to experience the joy that only you can bring.

*The LORD is my strength and shield.*
*I trust him with all my heart.*
*He helps me, and my heart is filled with joy.*
*I burst out in songs of thanksgiving.*

**PSALM 28:7**

THE Lord IS MY STRENGTH AND SHIELD

In the space below, illustrate or write down your feelings
about God's promise to never abandon you.

I WILL NEVER Abandon YOU

HEBREWS 13:5

57

# Don't Sweat
## THE SMALL STUFF

Father, I am often distracted by small matters
of injustice and give them much more attention than
they deserve. Help me remember that eventually every
knee will bow, every tongue will confess your greatness,
and every wrong will be made right.
Let me live in the security of knowing that you
will be victorious in the end.

*Who will not fear you, Lord, and glorify your name?*
*For you alone are holy. All nations will come*
*and worship before you, for your righteous*
*deeds have been revealed.*
**REVELATION 15:4**

# Glorify
## Your Name

# learn to
# DANCE
## in the Rain

*Lord,*

You are my shelter and refuge from life's storms. Knowing that you see each tear that falls and promise never to leave me brings such peace. Thank you for comforting me in the midst of my struggles and sorrows.

*He will wipe every tear from their eyes,*
*and there will be no more death or sorrow or crying or pain.*
*All these things are gone forever.*

REVELATION 21:4

# He will wipe
# EVERY TEAR

61

# THIS IS THE DAY THE

## *Lord has made*

Creator God,

Ah, what a glorious day to enjoy your creation. Thank you for giving us such a beautiful world in which to live this temporary life. I can only imagine what the next one holds. I pray that the works of your hands will continually point me to the wonders of your heart.

*O LORD, what a variety of things you have made!*
*In wisdom you have made them all.*

PSALM 104:24

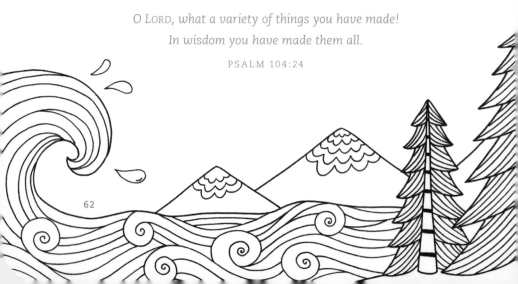

# YOU HAVE *Made* THEM ALL

# My friends and family who are far from God . . .

_____

_____

_____

_____

_____

Make a collage using pictures of family and friends whom you would like to pray for.

# NOBODY
*has to walk alone*

Lord,

You have placed me in this community for a reason. You know my neighbors by name and have a specific plan for each one. Help me see them through your eyes. May I reflect your comforting presence to those who are sad or lonely and offer your promise of rest to the burdened and weary. Please use me to demonstrate your extravagant love, no matter the need.

*I was hungry, and you fed me. I was thirsty, and you gave me a drink. I was a stranger, and you invited me into your home.*

MATTHEW 25:35

_____

_____

_____

_____

_____

*You*
INVITED ME
*into your home*

WELCOME

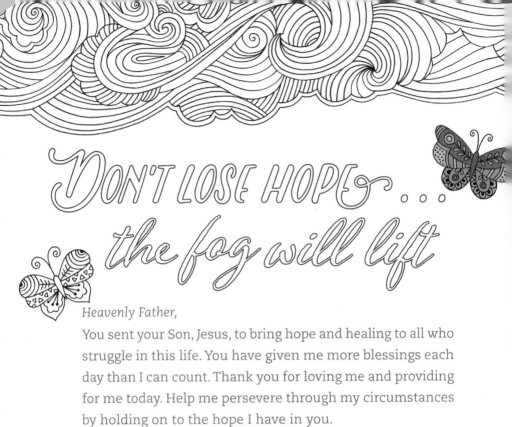

# Don't Lose Hope... the fog will lift

Heavenly Father,

You sent your Son, Jesus, to bring hope and healing to all who struggle in this life. You have given me more blessings each day than I can count. Thank you for loving me and providing for me today. Help me persevere through my circumstances by holding on to the hope I have in you.

*Love never gives up, never loses faith, is always hopeful,*
*and endures through every circumstance.*

1 CORINTHIANS 13:7

# home is where the HEART is

Lord Jesus,

Your Word reminds me that you had no earthly home of your own. I know that even now many of your followers around the globe struggle to find adequate shelter. I am so blessed that you have provided a safe haven for me. Forgive me for those times when I take it for granted and even envy those with bigger homes or "better" possessions.

*They were looking for a better place, a heavenly homeland.*
*That is why God is not ashamed to be called their God,*
*for he has prepared a city for them.*

HEBREWS 11:16

A heavenly homeland

Draw a map showing where you are called to make disciples.

# GO AND MAKE DISCIPLES

MATTHEW 28:19

# THE PURPOSE
## OF LIFE IS A LIFE OF
### *Purpose*

Lord,

I'm so thankful for this life! Today I'm going to enjoy reminders of the abundance you offer. You're my joy in the mundaneness of the everyday, my hope during tough times, my stability in a mixed-up world. When my patience wears thin, you infuse me with your strength. I praise you for every opportunity for your Spirit to work in mine. Thank you for salvation, Lord.

*The thief's purpose is to steal and kill and destroy.*
*My purpose is to give them a rich and satisfying life.*

JOHN 10:10

a rich and satisfying life

# FORGIVENESS IS A GIFT—NEVER TAKE IT FOR GRANTED

*Heavenly Father,*

Thank you for sending your Son to earth to pay for the penalty of my sin. I am overwhelmed with gratitude for your grace, and I long to share this gift with others. Could you help me not to overlook any opportunity to pass on the Good News of your Son to my loved ones today?

*There is one God and one Mediator who can reconcile God and humanity—the man Christ Jesus. He gave his life to purchase freedom for everyone.*

1 TIMOTHY 2:5-6

_____

_____

_____

_____

Lord,

Good news travels fast. Sharing a picture of a happy event takes only a moment. So why has so much time elapsed since I shared with others how grateful I am that you are in my life? Cultivate in me an excitement to shout my thanks to you from the mountaintops. May everyone I encounter hear the praise of your incomparable greatness on my lips.

*Give thanks to the Lord and proclaim his greatness.*
*Let the whole world know what he has done.*

PSALM 105:1

_____

_____

_____

_____

_____

_____

_____

_____

_____

_____

_____

# I GIVE these fears to God . . .

In the space below, make a list of your fears. Then cast your fears into the stream of living water and let God carry them away.

Failure

*Don't be afraid, for I am with you.* ISAIAH 41:10

Death

Rejection

*Those who drink the water I give will never be thirsty again. It becomes a fresh, bubbling spring within them, giving them eternal life.* JOHN 4:14

KEEP YOUR MOUTH SHUT AND YOUR

# Eyes Open

Lord,

If a picture is worth a thousand words, help me to be a picture of your character for others to observe. Close my mouth when necessary and help me live as an example of your holiness. Even when their ears are closed, may their eyes be open to notice you living in me.

*Let your good deeds shine out for all to see,*
*so that everyone will praise your heavenly Father.*

MATTHEW 5:16

# Shine

_____

_____

_____

_____

_____

_____

_____

_____

_____

_____

_____

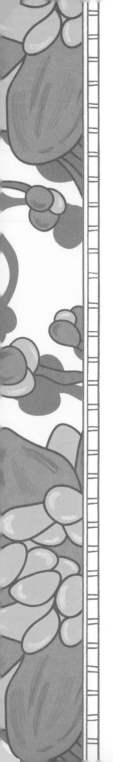

# *think*
# POSITIVE!

· · · · · · · · · · · · · · · · · · · · · · · · · · · · · ·

*Father,*

Will you please help me to balance living cautiously with embracing your heart of hope so I won't waste my energy with cynicism? If my hope really is in you and not in this shaky life, then I can hold to a positive outlook that reflects your truth.

*Let all that I am wait quietly before God,*
*for my hope is in him.*

PSALM 62:5

· · · · · · · · · · · · · · · · · · · · · · · · · · · · · · · · · · · · · · · · · · · · · · · ·

· · · · · · · · · · · · · · · · · · · · · · · · · · · · · · · · · · · · · · · · · · · · · · · ·

· · · · · · · · · · · · · · · · · · · · · · · · · · · · · · · · · · · · · · · · · · · · · · · ·

· · · · · · · · · · · · · · · · · · · · · · · · · · · · · · · · · · · · · · · · · · · · · · · ·

· · · · · · · · · · · · · · · · · · · · · · · · · · · · · · · · · · · · · · · · · · · · · · · ·

· · · · · · · · · · · · · · · · · · · · · · · · · · · · · · · · · · · · · · · · · · · · · · · ·

· · · · · · · · · · · · · · · · · · · · · · · · · · · · · · · · · · · · · · · · · · · · · · · ·

MY
HOPE
IS IN
HIM!

# He is the
# POTTER,
## and I am his
# CLAY

Lord,

You are the ultimate example for me. I long to reflect your character to others and invite you to shine through me more brightly than ever. Focus my thoughts on you so I can give up sinful habits and be molded and shaped into your likeness. Thank you for guiding my path!

*Let the Spirit renew your thoughts and attitudes.*
*Put on your new nature, created to be like God—*
*truly righteous and holy.*

EPHESIANS 4:23-24

# CREATED
## *to be like God*

_____

_____

_____

_____

_____

_____

_____

_____

*Journal about how this Scripture verse gives you hope,*
*or draw illustrations to express what these words mean to you.*

# performing for an AUDIENCE OF ONE ☦

Holy Spirit,

When I'm tempted to place my security in the approval of others, please remind me that *your* opinion is what matters. I desire your delight. Lord, would you fill my mouth with your praise? And guard my lips so each word spoken brings honor to you. Conform my reflections to the principles in your Word. Thank you, Lord, for being my solid ground and faithful helper.

*May the words of my mouth and the*
*meditation of my heart be pleasing to you, O LORD,*
*my rock and my redeemer.*

PSALM 19:14

my rock and my redeemer

# BEAR the BEST FRUIT

God,

Please bathe me in your truth, hope, patience, mercy, and gratitude. Transform the "less" of my mind and heart with the "more" of yourself. Clear away the weeds so the produce of your Spirit can thrive. Thank you for allowing me to feel restless until you work into me the growth I need. I want to be teachable so I can bless you and those you care about.

*The Holy Spirit produces this kind of fruit in our lives:*
*love, joy, peace, patience, kindness, goodness, faithfulness,*
*gentleness, and self-control.*

GALATIANS 5:22-23

love, JOY, PEACE, patience, KINDNESS, goodness, FAITHFULNESS, gentleness, AND SELF-Control

93

# follow the
## light
### unflinchingly

God,

I esteem you for treating your beloved children with care and compassion that is unique to each one. I'm grateful that you know the number of hairs on our heads. We have worth only because you, Lord, have bestowed it upon us. And with a shepherd's heart, you go before us, lighting the path ahead. May we follow you with bold trust, confident in your unfailing love.

*Long ago the LORD said to Israel: "I have loved you, my people, with an everlasting love. With unfailing love I have drawn you to myself."* JEREMIAH 31:3

# COUNT YOUR *Blessings*

Artfully illustrate the word Blessings in the space below.

# TAKE IT
## step by step

*Father,*

When I stop to count my innumerable blessings, I'm overwhelmed. You've been with me every step of my journey, and your unfailing love has never ceased. Thank you for adopting me as your very own child. My heart longs to trust you at a deeper level. Remind me to rejoice in the simple things. Fill my heart with joy and peace as I meditate on you today.

*You love him even though you have never seen him.*
*Though you do not see him now, you trust him; and*
*you rejoice with a glorious, inexpressible joy.*

1 PETER 1:8

**I AM UNIQUE; I AM SPECIAL; I AM ME**

God,

You created me exactly the way I am for a reason. Help me to let go of any preconceived notions of what I think I should be and instead look to you for guidance. Thank you for uniquely gifting me so I can fulfill the plans and purposes you have for my life. Help me find my worth and self-esteem in you rather than in worldly things.

*We are God's masterpiece.*
*He has created us anew in Christ Jesus,*
*so we can do the good things he planned for us long ago.*

EPHESIANS 2:10

# We are God's masterpiece

# WITH LOVE,
## there is no such thing as too much

Father,
I'm so grateful for the example of love you've given
me in the sacrifice of your Son, Jesus. You loved
me so much that you sent him to this earth so I
would have forgiveness and a close relationship
with you. Thank you that as I experience firsthand
your patience and kindness, I can exhibit that
same love to those you've placed in my life.

*Love is patient and kind.*
*Love is not jealous or boastful or proud or rude.*
*It does not demand its own way. It is not irritable,*
*and it keeps no record of being wronged.*

1 CORINTHIANS 13:4-5

PSALM 103:2

Draw a self-portrait in the space below as you consider
how you can praise God with your whole being.

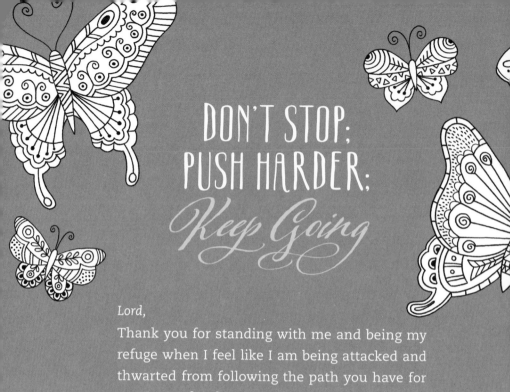

# DON'T STOP;
# PUSH HARDER;
## *Keep Going*

Lord,

Thank you for standing with me and being my refuge when I feel like I am being attacked and thwarted from following the path you have for me. I pray for the strength to continue to push forward when it feels too difficult. Please clear the way for me to take the next step. As I overcome each obstacle, I will be met with joy!

*Joyful are people of integrity,*
*who follow the instructions of the LORD.*
*Joyful are those who obey his laws and search*
*for him with all their hearts.*

PSALM 119:1-2

Joyful are
those who obey

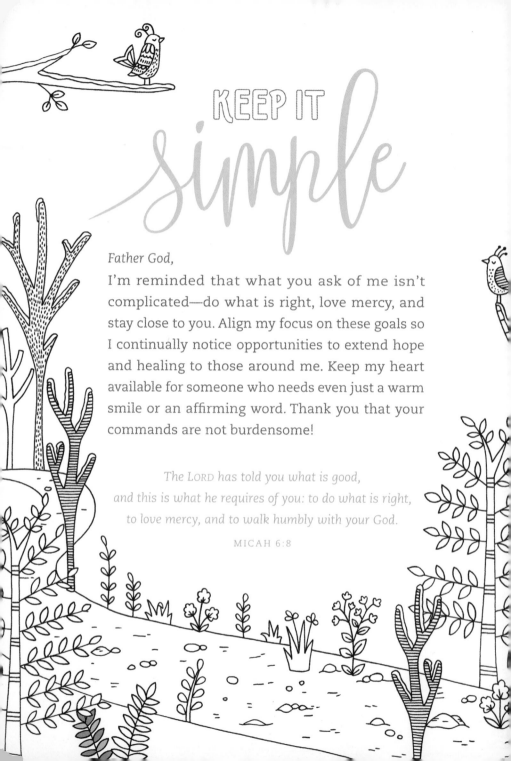

# KEEP IT *simple*

Father God,

I'm reminded that what you ask of me isn't complicated—do what is right, love mercy, and stay close to you. Align my focus on these goals so I continually notice opportunities to extend hope and healing to those around me. Keep my heart available for someone who needs even just a warm smile or an affirming word. Thank you that your commands are not burdensome!

*The LORD has told you what is good,*
*and this is what he requires of you: to do what is right,*
*to love mercy, and to walk humbly with your God.*

MICAH 6:8

walk
HUMBLY WITH YOUR
God

# NOTES

......................................................

......................................................

......................................................

......................................................

......................................................

......................................................

......................................................

......................................................

......................................................

......................................................

......................................................